Countries We Come From

Pakistan

by Rachel Anne Cantor

Consultant: Karla Ruiz, MA
Teachers College, Columbia University
New York, New York

BEARPORT PUBLISHING

New York, New York

Credits

Cover, © ZouZou/Shutterstock and © Shahid Khan/Shutterstock; TOC, © M.Khebra/Shutterstock; 4, © Jon Arnold Images Ltd/Alamy; 5T, © SunnyStock/Shutterstock; 5B, © naihei/Shutterstock; 7, © ameer_great/iStock; 8, © Asianet-Pakistan/Alamy; 9T, © Asia Images Group Pte Ltd/Alamy; 9B, © Imran Ahmed/Alamy; 10, © K_Boonnitrod/Shutterstock; 11, © Iryna Rasko/Shutterstock; 12, © OlegD/Shutterstock; 13T, © MZPHOTO.CZ/Shutterstock; 13B, © Iakov Filimonov/Shutterstock; 14–15, © Universal Images Group North America LLC/DeAgostini/Alamy; 15B, © robertharding/Alamy; 16L, © epa european pressphoto agency b.v./Alamy; 16–17, © Asianet-Pakistan/Shutterstock; 18, © Aman Ahmed Khan/Shutterstock; 19, © Florian Kopp/imageBROKER/AGE Fotostock; 20, © Hemis/Alamy; 21T, © Asianet-Pakistan/Shutterstock; 21B, © JOAT/Shutterstock; 22, © SMDSS/Shutterstock; 23, © espies/Shutterstock; 24, © dbimages/Alamy; 25T, © REUTERS/Alamy; 25B, © Georgejmclittle/Shutterstock; 26, © epa european pressphoto agency b.v./Alamy; 27, © Mai Groves/Shutterstock; 28L, © Pichugin Dmitry/Shutterstock; 28–29, © dbimages/Alamy; 30T, © Oleg_Mit/Shutterstock, © Andrey Lobachev/Shutterstock, and © ET1972/Shutterstock; 30B, © PACIFIC PRESS/Alamy; 31 (T to B), © Andrei Nekrassov/Shutterstock, © Patrick Poendl/Shutterstock, © Asianet-Pakistan/Shutterstock, © SunnyStock/Shutterstock, © suronin/Shutterstock, and © Bloomua/Shutterstock; 32, © Tim UR/Shutterstock.

Publisher: Kenn Goin
Editor: Jessica Rudolph
Creative Director: Spencer Brinker
Design: Debrah Kaiser
Photo Researcher: Thomas Persano

Library of Congress Cataloging-in-Publication Data

Names: Cantor, Rachel Anne, author.
Title: Pakistan / by Rachel Anne Cantor.
Other titles: Countries we come from.
Description: New York, New York : Bearpoint Publishing, 2017. | Series:
   Countries we come from | Includes bibliographical references and index.
Identifiers: LCCN 2016038808 (print) | LCCN 2016046865 (ebook) | ISBN
   9781684020607 (library) | ISBN 9781684021123 (ebook)
Subjects: LCSH: Pakistan—Juvenile literature.
Classification: LCC DS376.9 .C36 2017 (print) | LCC DS376.9 (ebook) | DDC
   954.91—dc23
LC record available at https://lccn.loc.gov/2016038808

For more information, write to Bearport Publishing Company, Inc., 45 West 21st Street, Suite 3B, New York, New York 10010. Printed in the United States of America.

10 9 8 7 6 5 4 3 2 1

Contents

HISTORIC

Friendly

WONDERFUL

Pakistan is a country in Asia.
About 200 million people live there.

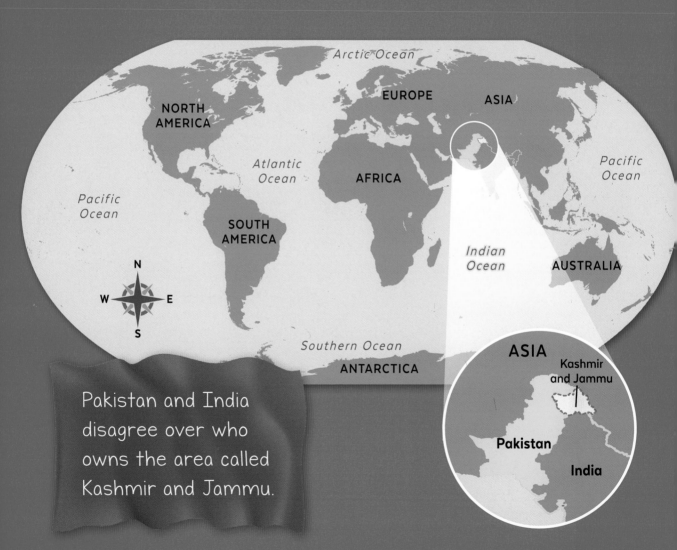

NORTH AMERICA

EUROPE

ASIA

Arctic Ocean

Atlantic Ocean

AFRICA

Pacific Ocean

Pacific Ocean

SOUTH AMERICA

Indian Ocean

AUSTRALIA

N
W   E
S

Southern Ocean

ANTARCTICA

ASIA

Kashmir and Jammu

Pakistan

India

Pakistan and India disagree over who owns the area called Kashmir and Jammu.

The **capital** of Pakistan is Islamabad.

The largest city is Karachi.

Karachi is home to more than 23 million people.

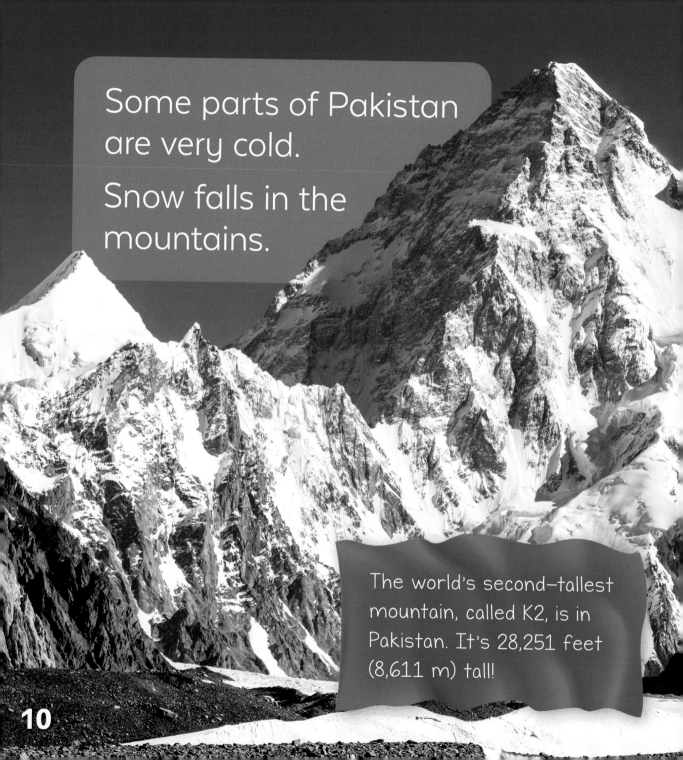

Some parts of Pakistan are very cold.

Snow falls in the mountains.

The world's second–tallest mountain, called K2, is in Pakistan. It's 28,251 feet (8,611 m) tall!

Other areas, such as the deserts, are hot.

Interesting animals live in Pakistan. Tall camels walk across the sandy deserts.

Leopard geckos crawl over rocks.

Markhors (MAHR-kawrz) climb mountains.

The markhor is a type of wild goat with thick, curly horns.

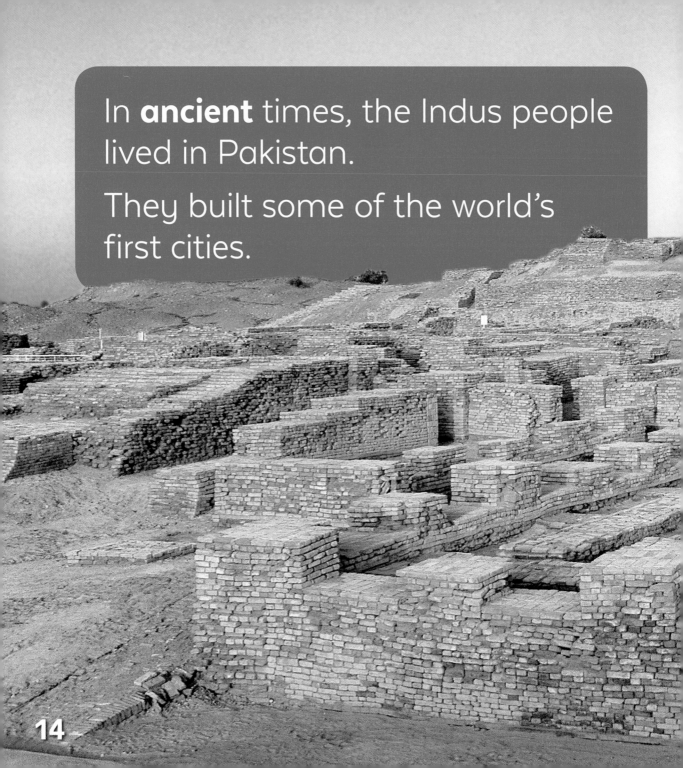

In **ancient** times, the Indus people lived in Pakistan.

They built some of the world's first cities.

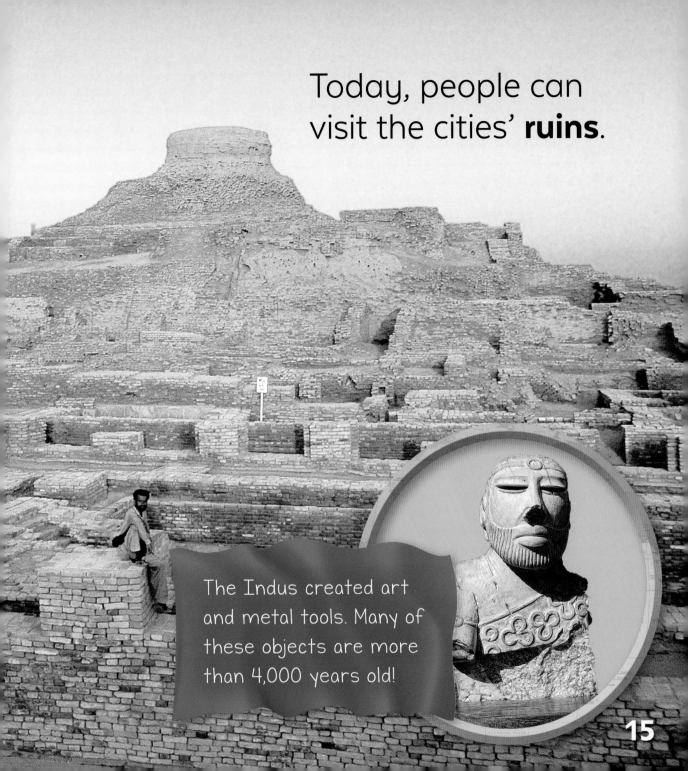

Today, people can visit the cities' **ruins**.

The Indus created art and metal tools. Many of these objects are more than 4,000 years old!

15

In the 1800s, Great Britain took control of much of southern Asia.

The people of Pakistan wanted their freedom.

In 1947, Pakistan became an **independent** country.

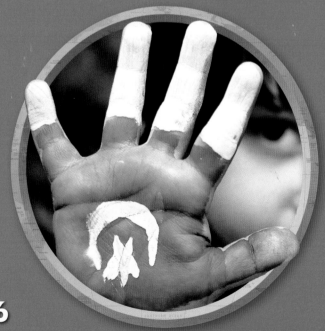

Pakistanis celebrate their freedom on August 14th.

17

Dozens of languages are spoken in Pakistan.

Many people speak Urdu.

This is how you say *thank you* in Urdu:

Shukria (SHOOK-ree-yah)

Many Pakistanis speak more than one language. Lots of people know English and Punjabi.

19

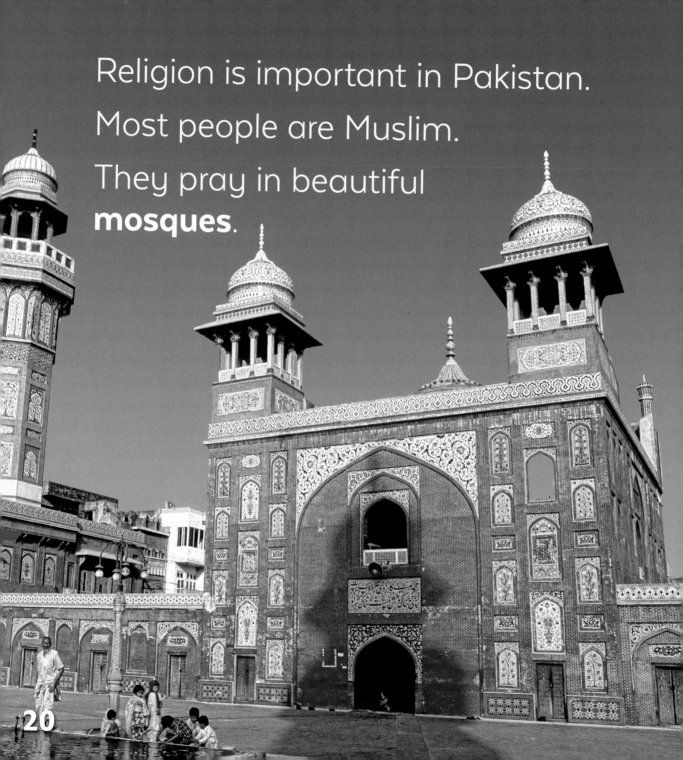

Religion is important in Pakistan.
Most people are Muslim.
They pray in beautiful
mosques.

One Muslim holiday is Eid al-Fitr (ID ahl-FIT-ur). Family members exchange gifts and eat tasty meals together.

Pakistanis make many delicious foods.

Biryani is a spicy rice dish.

Chicken, lamb, and vegetables are often added to the rice.

Many meals include a flat bread called roti.

Some Pakistanis work on farms.

a mustard farmer

24

Other people work in factories.

They make clothing and other products.

Many workers sell the latest **technology**, such as cell phones.

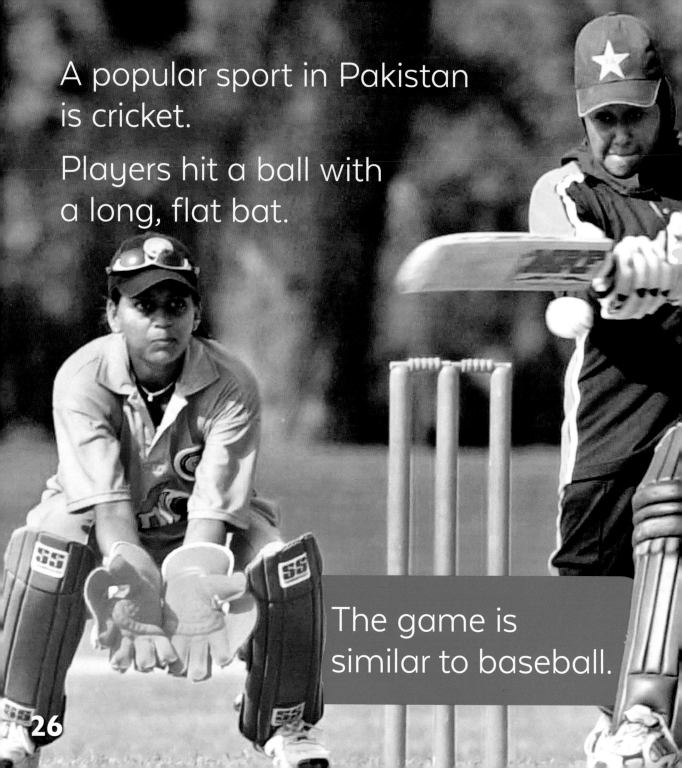

A popular sport in Pakistan is cricket.

Players hit a ball with a long, flat bat.

The game is similar to baseball.

Pakistan's national sport is field hockey.

27

In Pakistan, trucks and buses can be beautiful art!

Artists paint colorful designs on the trucks.

Some artists glue small mirrors to the trucks. The mirrors reflect sunlight to make the art look brighter.

Fast Facts

Capital city: Islamabad

Population of Pakistan: About 200 million

Main languages: Urdu, English, and Punjabi

Money: Pakistani rupee

Major religion: Islam

Neighboring countries: India, Afghanistan, Iran, and China

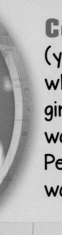

Cool Fact: Malala Yousafzai (yoo–sahf–ZEYE) is a Pakistani who works to make sure all girls can go to school. Malala won an award called the Nobel Peace Prize in 2014 when she was just 17 years old!

ancient (AYN-shunt) very old

capital (KAP-uh-tuhl) a city where a country's government is based

independent (in-duh-PEN-duhnt) free from control by others

mosques (MAHSKS) buildings used by Muslims for worship

ruins (ROO-inz) what is left of something that has decayed or been destroyed

technology (tek-NAHL-uh-jee) machinery and equipment developed with scientific knowledge

Index

Read More

Black, Carolyn. *Pakistan: The People.* New York: Crabtree (2003).

Sonneborn, Liz. *Pakistan (Enchantment of the World).* New York: Children's Press (2013).

Learn More Online

To learn more about Pakistan, visit
www.bearportpublishing.com/CountriesWeComeFrom

About the Author

Rachel Anne Cantor grew up in New Jersey and now lives in Massachusetts. She would love to visit Pakistan someday.